DESIGNING Healthy Communities

Design Thinking for a Better World

Sheri Doyle

CRABTREE
PUBLISHING COMPANY
WWW.CRABTREEBOOKS.COM

Author: Sheri Doyle

Series research and development:
Reagan Miller and Janine Deschenes

Editors: Janine Deschenes and Rachel Stuckey

Editorial director: Kathy Middleton

Editorial services: Clarity Content Services

Proofreader: Angela Kaelberer

Production coordinator and prepress technician:
Tammy McGarr

Print coordinator: Katherine Berti

Cover design: Tammy McGarr

Design: David Montle

Photo Research: Linda Tanaka

Photo Credits:
pp4-5 Photo courtesy of WE Charity, p5 Fred Lum/The Globe and Mail; p6 Rawpixel/shutterstock; p7 bitt24/shutterstock; p8 antoniodiaz/shutterstock; p9 Photos courtesy of Practical Action; p10 kittipong053/shutterstock; p11 Rawpixel/shutterstock; p12 antoniodiaz/shutterstock; p13 Joseph Thomas Photography/shutterstock; p14 ALPA PROD/shutterstock; p15 donatas1205/shutterstock; pp16-17 Sergey Novikov/shutterstock; pp18-19 Monkey Business Images/shutterstock; p19 Jacek Chabrazewski/shutterstock; p20 top muzsy/shutterstock, Steve Bridge/dreamstime; p21 CLS Digital Arts/shutterstock; p22 Andrey_Popov/shutterstock; p23 Antonio Guillem/shutterstock; p24 Lisa F. Young/shutterstock; p25 Sergey Novikov/shutterstock; p26 stockfour/shutterstock; p27 Rawpixel/shutterstock; p28 top bitt24/shutterstock, Brian A Jackson/shutterstock; p29 top USDA, AYA/shutterstock; p30 SpeedKingz/shutterstock; p31 Africa Studio/shutterstock; p32 Kurkul/shutterstock; p33 Photo courtesy of Practical Action; p34 Atstock Productions/shutterstock; p35 Rawpixel/shutterstock; p36 top greenaperture/shutterstock, kazoka/shutterstock; p37 top africa924/shutterstock, Sarine Arslanian/shutterstock; p38 The Canadian Press/Steve Lambert; p39 Linda Parton/shutterstock; p40 Barbara Kalbfleisch/shutterstock; p41 Jen Watson/shutterstock; p42 nikkytok/shutterstock; p43 Rawpixel/shutterstock; p44 left Monkey Business Images/shutterstock, Ricardo Mayer/shutterstock.

Library and Archives Canada Cataloguing in Publication

Doyle, Sheri, author
Designing healthy communities / Sheri Doyle.

(Design thinking for a better world)
Includes bibliographical references and index.
Issued in print and electronic formats.
ISBN 978-0-7787-4459-7 (hardcover).--
ISBN 978-0-7787-4463-4 (softcover).--ISBN 978-1-4271-2034-2 (HTML)

1. Community development--Health aspects--Juvenile literature. 2. Health planning--Social aspects--Juvenile literature. 3. Health promotion--Juvenile literature. 4. Public health--Juvenile literature. 5. Social participation--Juvenile literature. I. Title.

RA427.8.D69 2018 j362.1 C2017-908086-5
C2017-908087-3

Library of Congress Cataloging-in-Publication Data

Names: Doyle, Sheri, 1969- author.
Title: Designing healthy communities / Sheri Doyle.
Description: New York, New York : Crabtree Publishing Company, [2018] | Series: Design thinking for a better world | Includes bibliographical references and index.
Identifiers: LCCN 2017060079 (print) | LCCN 2018011638 (ebook) | ISBN 9781427120342 (Electronic) | ISBN 9780778744597 (hardcover) | ISBN 9780778744634 (pbk.)
Subjects: LCSH: Public health--Juvenile literature. | Nutrition policy--Juvenile literature. | Social planning--Juvenile literature.
Classification: LCC RA418 (ebook) | LCC RA418 .D697 2018 (print) | DDC 362.1/042--dc23
LC record available at https://lccn.loc.gov/2017060079

Crabtree Publishing Company
www.crabtreebooks.com 1-800-387-7650

Printed in the U.S.A./052018/CG20180309

Published in Canada
Crabtree Publishing
616 Welland Ave.
St. Catharines, Ontario
L2M 5V6

Published in the United States
Crabtree Publishing
PMB 59051
350 Fifth Avenue, 59th Floor
New York, New York 10118

Published in the United Kingdom
Crabtree Publishing
Maritime House
Basin Road North, Hove
BN41 1WR

Published in Australia
Crabtree Publishing
3 Charles Street
Coburg North
VIC, 3058

Contents

Designing Healthy Communities ... 4
The Design-thinking Process ... 6
Empathize ... 8
Define ... 10
Ideate ... 12
Prototype ... 14
Test ... 16
Reflect ... 18

PROJECT Need for Active Living ... 20
CASE Prolonged Sitting and Screen Time ... 22
CASE Fitness Programs for Every Body ... 23
CASE Not Enough Space for Physical Activity at School ... 25
DESIGN THINKING IN PRACTICE Being More Active ... 26

PROJECT Need for Healthy Food ... 28
CASE Access to Food in Local Communities ... 30
CASE Healthy Snack Options for Diabetic Students ... 31
CASE Hunger in Nepal ... 32
DESIGN THINKING IN PRACTICE Accessing Healthy Food ... 34

PROJECT Need for Clean Water ... 36
CASE Access to Clean Water at Shoal Lake 40 First Nation ... 38
CASE The Flint Water Crisis ... 39
CASE Need for Clean Water in Rwanda ... 41
DESIGN THINKING IN PRACTICE Accessing Clean Water ... 42

What's Next for Designing Healthy Communities? ... 44
Learning More ... 45
Bibliography ... 45
Glossary ... 47
Index ... 48
About the Author ... 48

Designing Healthy Communities

The Buzz about Design Thinking

People are using design thinking to improve lives and solve big problems around the world. Students have used design thinking to discover wonderful community solutions. For example, a design thinker who wants to encourage healthy living might create special exercise programs to get kids active at school. Design thinking offers limitless possibilities.

What Is Design Thinking?

Design thinking is a step-by-step **process** that helps designers solve problems. It inspires collaboration with others to find solutions, and active participation within our communities. To participate means to be involved in something. Design thinkers actively participate within a community to create solutions. At the center of design thinking is empathy, which is the ability to understand and share the feelings of others. In design thinking, we use empathy to understand the user's specific challenges, thoughts, and needs.

Who Is the User?

The user is the person or the group of people with a problem or need. A user could be a middle-school student with **diabetes** who needs better school lunch options. The user could also be a group of people, such as the survivors of a hurricane who require access to clean water and food.

How Design Thinkers Work

Through research, interviewing, and listening to the users, design thinkers develop a deep understanding of the users' challenges and their needs. Empathy is the driving force behind design thinking. Guided by empathy, design thinkers collaborate with the user to work through steps toward a solution. These steps involve trial and error. Mistakes are part of the creative process, and they often lead to better solutions.

Meet some CHANGE MAKERS

WE Charity and Clean Water in Communities

Craig and Marc Kielburger, the founders of WE Charity, use empathy to help improve the lives of people in communities around the world. They learn about the communities' needs, then work in partnership with those communities to create long-term solutions. In 2010, team members at the WE Charity went to the community of Dos Palais in Haiti to understand the needs of the people there. WE team members talked with the community members and asked questions about their needs. They learned that the elementary school was old and falling apart. The classrooms were leaky and overcrowded, and the teachers had few school supplies. It was hard for children to learn in these conditions. There were also many new students coming to the school after the major earthquake in 2010 destroyed over 4,000 other schools in Haiti, making the classrooms even more overcrowded. With this understanding, WE worked with the community to build a new elementary school for the children of Dos Palais and the others who had come after the earthquake. They also equipped, or provided, the school with supplies.

The Kielburger brothers attend WE Day events in many cities. This special event inspires young people to become change-makers in their community and around the world.

Haiti is the poorest country in the **Western Hemisphere** and most Haitians live in extreme poverty. In Dos Palais, most community members do not have jobs and have no way to earn money. To also help solve this problem, the WE team hired local workers to build the schools. Because the WE team used empathy to understand the different needs of the Dos Palais community, they were able to create a solution that could help its many members.

In Dos Palais, each part of the school is painted a different color. When students were asked what color they would like to paint the school, each grade chose a different color of the rainbow!

The Design-thinking Process

The design-thinking process is a set of steps that support creative problem solving. There are different versions of the process, but all of them start with empathy and putting the user's needs first. In this book, you will follow these steps to develop user-centered solutions.

We explore this process throughout the book to help you be a design thinker. The steps are iterative. This means they are repeated many times until a solution is found.

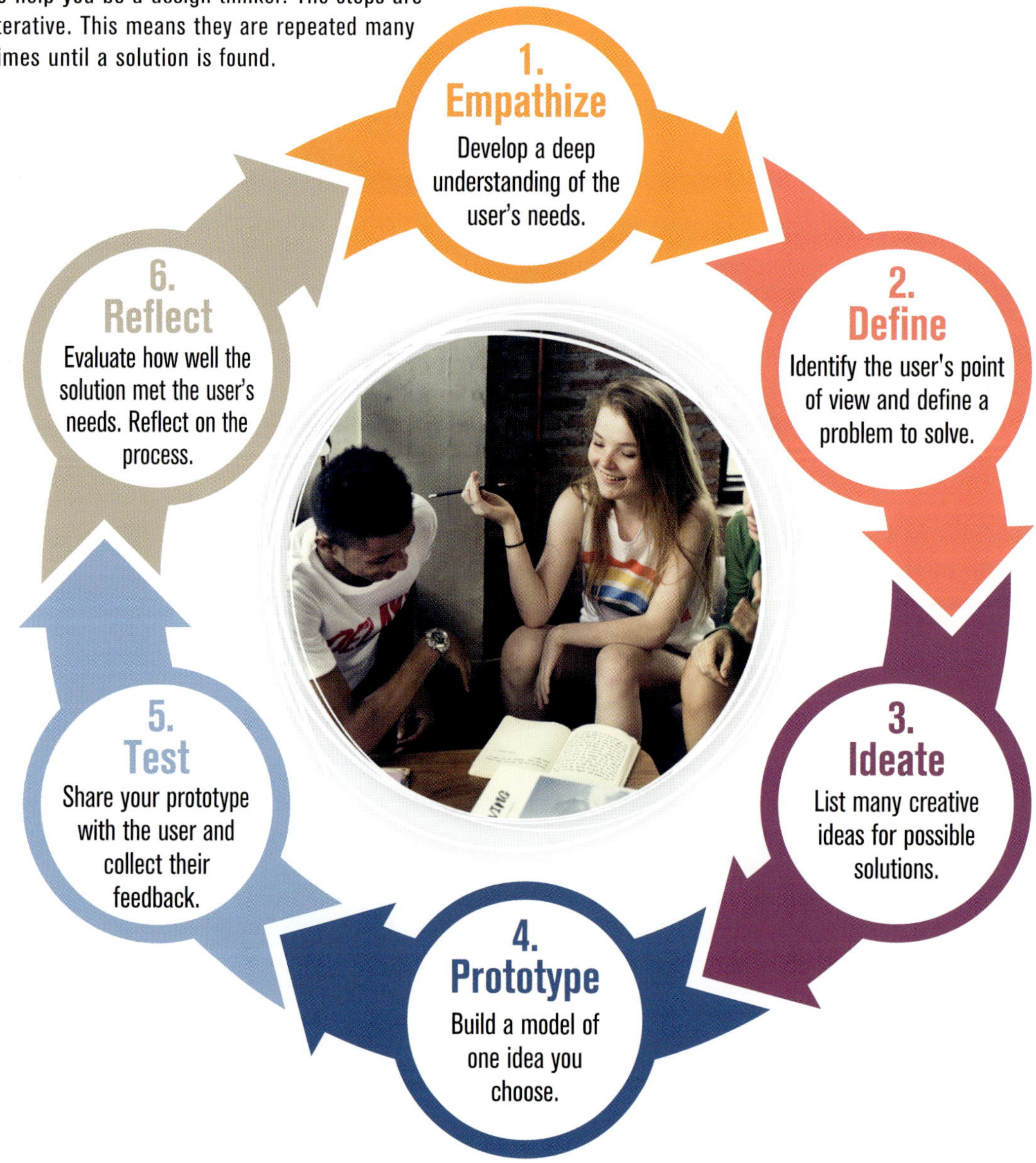

What Is a Community?

A community is a group of people who live, work, and play in a place. In a healthy community, people have access to the things they need to keep their bodies and minds in good health, including exercise, food, and clean water.

Some people face challenges in their communities that put their health at risk. For example, natural disasters such as hurricanes and flooding can block people's access to safe food and water. A lack of space or programming can make it difficult for people to stay fit and active. Design thinking can create solutions to these problems.

In a healthy community, everyone has access to plenty of fresh, whole foods. Communities in remote places often do not have the same access to a variety of foods that people in populated places do. They may have to grow their own food or rely on buying unhealthy, processed food.

This book features case studies about barriers that impede people's ability to live healthily. By using the design-thinking steps, you will be able to understand the needs of these people and work toward solutions.

Mindset Tips

Stay Open	When working in a group, keep an open mind about the ideas of others.
Dig Deeper	If you don't understand something a group member is trying to say, ask questions.
Take Turns	Let all members of the group have a chance to share ideas and ask questions.
Share	Think about and share your own memories and experiences to relate to ideas and get around roadblocks during the design-thinking process.
Pace It	Keep track of the time during every aspect of the process.

Empathize

What Is Empathy?

Empathy is the ability to understand and share the feelings of others. Building empathy is the most important step in design thinking. When users share their point of view, design thinkers can gain a deeper understanding of the users' needs. Design thinkers try to understand the user's experiences and imagine what it's like to live in the user's world.

Design thinkers can build empathy for their user by engaging with them: asking questions, seeking answers, and listening.

How Do We Build Empathy?

Design thinkers use different strategies to build empathy. Sometimes, design thinkers can get to know users by visiting them in their community. Other times, design thinkers do research to learn about a user they cannot meet in person. Some strategies to help you practice empathy include:

- **Immerse** yourself in the user's life through their own words, photos, or recordings.
- **Engage** by asking questions, seeking answers, and listening.
- **Observe** by taking a step back to watch, take in, and think.

Engaging to Build Empathy

Before you meet with the user or begin your research, write down as many questions as you can. Put your best questions in an order that makes sense, grouping related questions together.

Possible questions might include:

- Can you tell me about the healthy choices you make in your life?
- What healthy choices do you want to make?
- What challenges or barriers do you face when making healthy choices?
- Why do you think these barriers exist?
- How does this problem make you feel?
- What are some solutions that you have thought about?

Meet some CHANGE MAKERS

Practical Action in Bangladesh

Innovators at an organization called Practical Action used empathy to help people living in poverty in the country of Bangladesh. First, they learned how flooding in agricultural communities caused food shortages. They understood that flooded land meant that people could not grow the food they needed to survive. With the needs of these people in mind, Practical Action designed floating gardens to help solve the problem. Now, people can grow food on flooded land. Practical Action worked directly with the people of Bangladesh, putting their needs at the heart of the solution.

These floating gardens are a user-centered solution to the problem of flooded farmland in Bangladesh.

What Is the Need of the User?

After you use empathy to understand the user's problem, you must define their specific need. To do this, you will need to **synthesize** the information you learned in the empathy stage. This means that you bring together all the information you collected. Here are some methods for synthesizing the information you collected:

- Use sticky notes to record each fact, thought, or feeling the user shared.
- Create an empathy map by dividing a piece of paper into four sections. In each section record something the user 1) said, 2) felt, 3) thought, and 4) did.
- Create a journey map to record a user's experience over time, such as a day in their life.

Point of View

Let's say a group of middle-school students have shared how they don't like their cafeteria's food because it's greasy, tastes bad, and gives them stomachaches. Without a healthy and tasty lunch, they have difficulty concentrating in class.

One way to synthesize your information is to record each observation on a sticky note and then organize the notes.

After design thinkers synthesize the information they gather in the empathy stage, they use a point-of-view question to define the problem.

Design thinkers can use a point-of-view (POV) statement to describe the user and their need. First, clearly define the user. In this case, the users are middle-school students who eat lunch at their school's cafeteria. Next, define the user's specific need by referring back to the users' thoughts and opinions shared during the empathy stage. In this case, the middle-school students need healthy and tasty food to eat in their lunch cafeteria.

Point-of-View Question

Once a design thinker has identified the user and their need in a POV statement, they may create a POV question, which helps define the problem they will solve. In the example of the middle-school students, you might ask this POV question: "How can we improve the students' access to healthy food?"

Getting Started

Use these prompts to help draft a POV question:

- How can we help ...?
- How can we create a way to ...?
- How can we improve ...?
- How can we prevent ...?
- How might we ...?

Why Is the Define Step Important?

This step helps you pinpoint the problem that the user faces. By defining the user's need, you can create a question that points to a solution. The define step helps move you from thought to action.

Ideate

What Is Ideation?

Ideation means forming ideas. In the ideation step, you **brainstorm** possible solutions to your user's problem. Brainstorming helps to answer your POV question by thinking openly to identify ideas big and small, practical and wild. One idea that seems silly might be the idea that gets you thinking about a very useful solution.

Why Is Ideation Important?

Ideation allows design thinkers the freedom to explore many possible solutions and weigh the potential success of each one. Ideation works best in a group because our ideas become stronger when we think and ideate together.

One problem may have many possible solutions. A solution can be a product or a process. A product is a physical object, such as the school that WE Charity built for students in Haiti. A process is a way of doing something. For example, an exercise schedule could be a process solution to someone who has trouble staying active.

Here are some methods to help you get some ideas flowing:

- Brainstorm—write ideas on a chalkboard, whiteboard, or paper.
- Use visuals such as drawings.
- Set rules such as "stay on topic" or "wild ideas only."
- Brainstorm visually through pictures.

TIPS:
Hydration Ideation!

Let's say a group of design thinkers have worked through the empathy and define steps on the issue of students not drinking enough water. They created this POV question: How can students increase their water intake during the school day? They brainstorm the following ideas on a whiteboard:

- a Drink More Water campaign with informative flyers and posters
- a Drink More Water event day to raise awareness
- student **survey** "Are you getting enough water?" and blog with tips for getting more water
- installing more water fountains
- a visual schedule that shows more water breaks during the day
- a buzzer that will remind students to drink water

Make a Choice

After brainstorming, you must choose a few ideas to focus on. Set a time limit for this task. Strategies you could use to make a decision include ranking the options or listing the pros and cons of each idea.

Prototype

What Is a Prototype?

A prototype is a model or representation of an idea. The prototype is a "working" model, not a finished product, so it should be inexpensive, simple, and quick to build.

A prototype can be a product, such as a water-bottle carrier or a website, or a process, such as an event or a new type of exercise. If the prototype is a product, design thinkers build a model of it. If it is a process, design thinkers might create a **storyboard**, presentation, recording, or **role-play** to show their idea. The prototype is designed with the intention that it will be tested in the next step, ideally with the user.

Why Is a Prototype Important?

A prototype helps you show the user your idea. A prototype can also spark more questions about the idea or reveal mistakes. Prototypes help designers recognize an idea's strengths and weaknesses.

Time for Prototyping!

You've chosen an idea. It's time to build or create a prototype. Set a time limit, but allow yourself a little more time for this step than the others. If your solution is a product, you'll need to gather materials to build a model. If your solution is a process, you can use a storyboard or other visual organizer (such as paper or sticky notes) to show the idea.

You might need to gather supplies to create your prototype.

A design thinking prototype is a quick, inexpensive way to bring your idea to life. Try to use everyday materials that are easy to find. This is important because you may be creating many prototypes as you improve your solution!

Take time to make a list of needed supplies. Draw some designs of the physical model to help you plan. Physical models are likely to require more materials such as cardboard boxes of many sizes, plastic containers, and straws. You may also need supplies to shape materials (such as scissors) and supplies to attach them together (such as tape, glue, or a stapler).

TIPS: Act It Out!

If your idea is a process, such as an "awareness day" or an obstacle course, you can act it out for your prototype. Create the scenario of your idea. Assign roles, take turns improvising, use dialogue, or write a short script.

Test

What Is the Test Step?

Testing the prototype allows designers to see how well their solution may work for the user. As the user interacts with the prototype, designers learn whether the product or process is successful and get feedback from the user.

Ideally, users will try out the prototype, but this isn't always possible. Testers can be your peers or classmates. If the user is unavailable, explain to testers what you learned during the empathy step and share your POV statement and question.

TIPS:
How to Test

- Show, don't tell—Allow the testers to experience the prototype for themselves.
- Demonstrate—A quick demonstration may be needed to show testers how the prototype works.
- Share stories—Introduce the prototype with a short, meaningful story about it.
- Mimic—Set up tests so they mimic real-world scenarios.

If your target users are not available, you can test your prototype with your peers or classmates.

Failing Forward: What Tests Reveal

When users test the prototype, they may ask questions the design thinkers have not considered. Testing also reveals problems with the idea. The product or process could even fail, but this allows design thinkers to go back to the beginning to improve on the idea. Mistakes will happen, but that's what **failing forward** is all about. Failure is a helpful part of moving forward in the design-thinking process, because it allows design thinkers to learn more and improve an idea.

Why It's Important to Test the Prototype

Receiving feedback helps designers understand their prototype from different perspectives. Tests help shed light on the strengths and weaknesses of the prototype. Feedback gives designers a chance to improve the design for the user.

Feedback

You can learn what worked and what needs improvement by:

- Listening to the words, comments, and questions of testers
- Observing testers' actions and behaviors while they try out the prototype
- Provide surveys for testers to fill out, then analyze answers on feedback surveys that users or testers fill out

Surveys for Feedback

A survey is a questionnaire that users fill out after they test the prototype. You can study and analyze the answers to help refine your design. Here are some questions you might want to include in a survey:

- Was it easy to use?
- Did you find the prototype helpful? If so, how?
- Did anything about the prototype surprise you?
- What might you change about the prototype?

Reflect

What Is Reflection?

Reflection is the final step in the design-thinking process. It helps design thinkers understand if and how the prototype met the needs of the user. Think back to the first and second steps—empathy and define—and remember the feelings, thoughts, problems, and needs of the user. Did the prototype fulfill the user's needs?

What worked? What didn't work? Reflection allows designers time to consider whether the design should be refined or if they should start again.

Why Is Reflection Important?

By thinking back through the steps of the process, designers can make sure that the user's needs are the focus of the project from start to finish. Reflection also allows us to think about how we can improve our design-thinking process. What worked well in each step and what could we do to make our process better?

How to Reflect

Try some of these tips to start your reflection:

- Write a list of the positive things users and others said about your prototype.
- Write a list of the ways the prototype could be improved based on feedback.
- Record any ideas that occurred to you during your presentation.
- Share your reflections with others.
- Listen to your peers' reflections. How are they similar to or different from your reflections?
- Write a reflection journal entry.

Design thinkers use feedback from testers to help them understand if their prototype met the needs of the users.

Writing a journal entry can help you reflect on the design-thinking process.

TIPS: Using Questions to Reflect

Try some of these questions to prompt your reflection:

- How was the prototype meaningful to the user?
- Did the prototype meet the user's need?
- Did the prototype do what I expected it to?
- What, if anything, was surprising about the prototype?
- How can I improve the prototype?

PROJECT:

Need for Active Living

Community activities are a great way to get some exercise.

What Is Physical Activity?

You are physically active when you are moving your body in some way. Physical activity should include **aerobic** activity such as dancing or jogging, muscle-strengthening activity such as push-ups and sit-ups, and bone-strengthening activity, such as rope jumping and basketball.

Physical activity helps people keep their heart and lungs healthy, build muscle, maintain a healthy weight, and reduce the risk of some diseases. It also helps keep us in good mental health. The U.S. Department of Health and Human Services says that children and adolescents need 60 minutes or more of physical activity daily.

In a healthy community, all members have the opportunity to participate in physical activity.

Why Don't People Always Meet Their Physical Activity Needs?

People can face many challenges that stop them from getting enough physical activity. Their job may require them to sit at a desk or in front of screens for long periods of time. Many people have trouble finding the time to be active, or they don't have the motivation or confidence to join in. Fitness programs can also be very expensive or too far away from home to be accessible. Persons with **disabilities** have fewer options for being physically active. And some communities simply don't have good quality recreation centers or safe parks for members to use for physical activities.

Meet some CHANGE MAKERS

This Girl Can!

The team at the British organization Sport England used empathy to understand why some girls and women feel uncomfortable participating in physical activity. They spoke with women and girls about what stops them from participating in sports and fitness activities, and discovered that the "fear of being judged" was the most common. Based on the feedback they received, the organization started a campaign called This Girl Can. The campaign promotes fitness in communities by hosting events that get girls and women interested in sports and fitness. It includes a website that educates and motivates girls and women to do the physical activities they love or want to try. This Girl Can puts users' needs first by inspiring women and girls to enjoy fitness without feeling judged about their bodies or abilities.

By spreading positive messages on social media, This Girl Can helps girls and women become more confident about physical activity.

CASE

Prolonged Sitting and Screen Time

Like many teens, 15-year-old Josh spends long hours sitting in front of a screen. After school, he does homework on his computer, enjoys television shows, plays video games, watches videos on his phone, and texts his friends often. Josh spends most of his screen time seated at a desk or lying on the couch.

While Josh enjoys his screen time, he's noticed that he has been feeling tired and his back muscles hurt. In gym class, he is not running as fast or for as long as he did when he made the track team last year. He feels embarrassed about being out of shape. He dreams of joining the track team again, but thinks he won't do well at tryouts this year. He doesn't want to stop playing video games, watching his favorite television shows and videos, and texting his friends. But he isn't sure how to balance all of his interests.

Only 27 percent of high school students met the guideline for engaging in one hour of physical activity daily, according to The Youth Risk Behavior Surveillance—United States, 2015.

Many teens, like Josh, are spending more time on screens and less time exercising.

- Teens who watch more than 5 hours of television daily are 5 times more likely to be overweight than those who watch 0 to 2 hours daily.
- Approximately 75 percent of teens have a smartphone.
- Four out five family homes have a device for video games.

The Design-thinking Process

Empathy What is Josh's barrier to regular exercise? How does his situation make him feel?

Define POV After you have used empathy to understand Josh's point of view, define his needs. Create a POV question that helps you begin to solve his problem.

POV QUESTION PROMPT: **How can we help ... ?**

CASE

Fitness Programs for Every Body

Thirteen-year-old Kate loves hip-hop dance. She is a great dancer, but after two years in dance club, she decided not sign up again. Kate was born with **spina bifida**, so she wears a leg brace.

Because of this, there are some moves that she cannot do, such as skipping or running across the stage. The teacher allowed her to make up her own steps during the parts that were difficult for her. But Kate felt singled out doing different moves than everyone else and wished her dance teacher provided more options. Kate has ideas for more inclusive choreography, but she was afraid that the other dancers would not like her ideas. Kate feels frustrated at school when her friends go to dance club. She used to feel energized and cheerful after dance club. Now she feels tired and sad after school.

Kate quit dance club because she did not feel included.

Did You Know?

Kate is not alone.

- About 25 percent of persons with disabilities say that they are not active, compared to just 13 percent of people who do not have disabilities.
- The **obesity** rate is almost 40 percent higher in students with disabilities.
- Research shows that students with disabilities who want to participate in sports often face negative attitudes and a lack of acceptance.

Participating in physical activity is a challenge for many people with disabilities. Because people have a wide range of physical abilities, we need to develop unique and adaptable activities that encourage participation for all.

The Design-thinking Process

Empathy What is stopping Kate from participating in dance club at school? How does sitting on a bench instead of participating in dance club make her feel?

Define POV After you have used empathy to understand Kate's point of view, define her needs. Create a POV question that helps you begin to solve her problem.

POV QUESTION PROMPT: **How could we provide ... ?**

CASE

Not Enough Space for Physical Activity at School

A group of middle-school students and their teachers are frustrated by the lack of space for physical activity at their school. They are not getting enough daily physical activity.

They share the school yard with younger students, so for safety reasons there are many activities they can't do at recess. The students wish they had had a sports field and track, like the high school students on the other side of the school fence. Their teachers have trouble scheduling time in the small gym they share with so many other classes. Students believe that they would benefit from more fitness activities. They say they need breaks from sitting at desks. There are plans to renovate the school, but that doesn't help solve the problem students face right now.

Did You Know?

Many young people don't have the space they need to stay active.

- Research shows that large spaces allow students to engage in more physical activity.
- A 2015 report shows that 435 New York City schools don't have a gym or space for physical activity.
- Research also shows that not having changing rooms and bike storage space makes it hard for students to be active.

The Design-thinking Process

Empathy What is holding back these middle-school students from enjoying physical fitness daily? How does their situation make them feel? What do the students and teachers wish for?

Define POV After you have used empathy to understand the middle-school students' point of view, define their needs. Create a POV question that helps you begin to solve their problem.

POV QUESTION PROMPT: **How could we improve ... ?**

Design Thinking in Practice

Being More Active

How can we help people to become more physically active?

It's time to put design thinking to work. Take a look back at the three users facing problems in this section:

1. Josh is out of shape and spends too much time sitting in front of screens. He enjoys playing video games, watching TV, and using his phone, but he needs more physical activity in his day.
2. Kate didn't sign up for dance club because when her disability prevented her from doing some dance moves, she felt left out. She does not feel that others will support her suggestions for different dance moves.
3. The students at the middle school don't have enough space for physical activity and must share the small space they have with a large number of younger students.

The U.S. Department of Health and Human Services recommends children and teens get at least 60 minutes of physical activity every day. It helps you stay healthy, focus in school, and develop skills like perseverance and teamwork.

Which student or group would you like to help? Choose either Josh, Kate, or the middle-school students' case and use the design-thinking steps to create a solution to their problem.

Empathize

Empathize to learn more about the user's point of view:

- Ask questions about their needs.
- Learn more by watching videos and reading articles.

Define

Use the POV prompt from the case study to define your user's need.

Ideate

It's time to brainstorm! Draw, sketch, or write down as many ideas as possible.
Organize your ideas and select one for the next stage.

Prototype

Create a prototype of your idea—keep it simple, cheap, and easy.
Remember that your prototype should be an experience.

Test

Show, don't tell—test your prototype with your peers to get feedback.

Reflect

Reflect on the results of your test.

- Has your prototype met the needs of the user?
- What can you change?

Reflect on the design-thinking process.

- What did you learn?
- What could you do differently?

Now, improve your prototype through another iteration of the process. When you are happy with your solution, share it with your peers.

PROJECT:

Need for Healthy Food

Food for Healthy Bodies

We need to eat a variety of healthy foods so that our bodies can work the way that they should. Healthy foods contain the **nutrients** our bodies need. We also need to eat the right amount of food to give us energy throughout the day.

Whole foods are natural foods full of nutrients that have not been changed with added sugar and salt. Examples include fruit, vegetables, grains, beans, fish, meats, eggs, cheese, and olive oil. The food we eat creates energy for our bodies. We feel our best when we eat the right amounts of healthy foods, including whole foods.

People who do not eat the right amount of healthy food may feel tired, weak, and have trouble fighting off disease. Eating too much or too little food can also make us feel this way. Processed food, such as potato chips and cookies, is food that has been changed by adding things such as unhealthy fats, salt, and sugar. A diet based on processed food, such as junk food, is unhealthy.

Access to Food

In a healthy community, healthy food is easy to grow or buy. For example, people are able to grow food if they have good quality land, access to water, and the right weather conditions. People can also buy food when they have money and can easily access grocery stores or markets.

People can read nutrition fact labels and ingredient lists to make informed food choices. When a choice is informed, it means that the person knows and understands information about it before choosing.

What prevents people from eating enough healthy food?

In many parts of the world, people do not have enough food. Hunger affects 815 million people around the world. For these people, healthy food may not be available where they live. Climate and weather may make it difficult to grow food. Many people throughout the world do not have enough money for food.

Some people have easier access to unhealthy food than to healthy food. They may buy junk food because it's cheaper than healthier food. **Malnutrition** can occur in people who do not eat enough food and also in those who eat too much unhealthy food.

Governments have many resources to help people make informed choices about the foods they eat.

Meet a CHANGE MAKER

Katie's Krops Feed the Community

Katie's Krops is an organization of young people helping to end hunger in their community. They grow vegetable gardens and use the food they grow to prepare and serve dinners to people in need. At age 9, Katie, the organization's founder, grew a 40-pound cabbage, which she gave to a soup kitchen. That cabbage helped feed 275 people! Through this experience, Katie learned that many people in her community did not have enough food to eat. When the only soup kitchen in her community closed, she knew that these people's needs were not being met. So, she started Katie's Krops Dinner. The organization provides a monthly dinner, using food from their own harvests, for people in her community. Katie continues to build empathy for the people by getting to know them.

A neighborhood garden is a user-focused solution for communities that have limited access to healthy food.

CASE

Access to Food in Local Communities

Mia, Chad, and their toddler son live in Buffalo, New York. They are hungry most of the time. Ever since Chad was laid off from his job, the family has had to rely on Mia's part-time income. It's not enough to cover rent and other expenses, and they often go without food.

Chad is working hard to find a job, and Mia has asked her employer for more shifts. Most of their money goes to paying the rent. They buy mostly inexpensive canned food and bread, when it's on sale. Mia and Chad feel hungry and tired all the time because the food they can afford doesn't fuel their bodies well. They are always worried about feeding their child and themselves enough food. They are scared and don't know where to access help.

Mia and Chad are often forced to buy inexpensive, processed foods. They cannot afford to buy healthy, whole foods, and sometimes they run out of food.

Did You Know?

Many North American families face hunger.

- Hunger affects 41 million Americans and 4 million Canadians.
- The 13 million children who face hunger in the United States are at a greater risk of health problems and more likely to struggle in school than students who eat well.
- In Canada, over one-third of people who get help from food banks are under 18 years old.

The Design-thinking Process

Empathy How do Mia, Chad, and their son face barriers to accessing healthy food? How does their situation make them feel?

Define POV After you have used empathy to understand the family's point of view, define their needs. Create a POV question that helps you begin to solve their problem.

POV QUESTION PROMPT: **How can we help ... ?**

CASE

Healthy Snack Options for Diabetic Students

Gabriella is a 14-year-old with **type 2 diabetes**, which means that she must eat a healthy diet that is low in sugar and unhealthy fats in order to control the disease. Gabriella knows which foods are healthiest for managing her **blood sugar** levels and weight.

Gabriella must eat a healthy diet to manage her diabetes. Most schools offer lunches with healthy options, but they still include many processed foods on the menu.

Most days she packs healthy lunches. There are also healthy options at the cafeteria such as grilled chicken and fresh salads. But at drama parties, student council events, and after soccer games, the snacks provided are usually pizza, chips, and cupcakes. Her doctor advises against eating these types of foods. Gabriella feels left out and frustrated when she can't enjoy the same snacks as her friends. She thinks people don't really understand what it's like to have type 2 diabetes. She wishes the snacks were healthier so she could enjoy them too.

Gabriella is not alone.

- About 30 million people have diabetes in the United States.
- Researchers in the University of Oxford's Health Experiences Research Group interview young people who have diabetes. Some participants described being left out of school trips and sports because of the risks associated with their diabetes.
- Diabetes can lead to major health problems such as heart attacks, stroke, kidney failure, and blindness.

The Design-thinking Process

Empathy What is stopping Gabriella from enjoying snacks served at school events? How does Gabriella feel about those snacks served?

Define POV After you have used empathy to understand Gabriella's point of view, define her needs. Create a POV question that helps you begin to solve her problem.

POV QUESTION PROMPT: **How might we ... ?**

CASE

Hunger in Nepal

Mana and her family live in Nepal, a country in South Asia. They rely on farming to grow the food they eat. Like many other families, they struggle to grow enough food to feed themselves. There are no markets or stores nearby where she could buy food, if she had the money.

With limited water for farming, many people in Nepal struggle to grow enough food for their families.

Among other problems, rainfall is inconsistent or unreliable, so the crops do not always have the water they need to grow. Mana and her children feel hungry and tired most of the time. They live in one of the poorest areas of Nepal. Her husband must travel to India to work, leaving Mana alone to look after the children and try to run the farm. When the rain stops, they often go hungry. Mana wishes they could have a consistent supply of water for their farm. She wishes that one day all their hard work will provide enough food for the family. She wishes that the hunger pains would go away.

Mana's family is among many who face hunger in Nepal.

- In Nepal, about 5 million people experience hunger.
- Almost 30% of children under the age of 5 suffer from malnutrition in Nepal.
- Because of poverty, many people in Nepal depend on growing their own food for survival.

The Design-thinking Process

Empathy What barriers to food access do Mana and her family face? How does Mana feel about her family's situation?

Define POV After you have used empathy to understand Mana's point of view, define her needs. Create a POV question that helps you begin to solve her problem.

POV QUESTION PROMPT: **How can we help ... ?**

Design Thinking in Practice

Accessing Healthy Food

How can we help people have access to healthy food?

It's time to put design thinking to work. Take a look back at the three users facing problems in this section:

1. Mia, Chad, and their toddler son in Buffalo, New York, are facing hunger. They can only afford small amounts of unhealthy packaged food.
2. Gabriella has type 2 diabetes and cannot enjoy the snacks served at school events. She feels left out and would like people to understand more about diabetes.
3. Mana and her family in Nepal face hunger because they don't have enough reliable water to grow food crops.

In North America, most people buy healthy food from grocery stores. Some people in North America cannot afford the cost of healthy, unprocessed food like this.

Which student or family would you like to help? Choose either Mia and Chad, Gabriella, or Mana's case and use the design-thinking steps to create a solution to their problem.

Empathize

Empathize to learn more about the user's point of view:

- Examine their stories, challenges, and frustrations.
- Learn more by watching videos and reading articles.

Define

Use the POV prompt from the case study to define your user's need.

Ideate

It's time to brainstorm! Draw, sketch, or write down as many ideas as possible. Organize your ideas and select one for the next stage.

Prototype

Create a prototype of your idea—keep it simple, cheap, and easy. Remember that your prototype should be an experience.

Test

Show, don't tell—test your prototype with your peers to get feedback

Reflect

Reflect on the results of your test.

- Has your prototype met the needs of the user?
- What can you change?

Reflect on the design-thinking process.

- What did you learn?
- What could you do differently?

Now, improve your prototype through another iteration of the process. When you are happy with your solution, share it with your peers.

PROJECT:

Need for Clean Water

Water and Human Health

Water makes up about 60 percent of human body weight. Every system in our bodies uses water. Although humans can survive for a few weeks without food, we cannot survive more than a few days without water.

Our Daily Water Needs

The amount of water humans need depends on age, weight, gender, level of activity, and climate. Teens and preteens should drink at least six to eight cups of water per day. When we sweat, we lose water. This means that in hot and humid weather, we need to drink more. When participating in physical activity, we need to take breaks to drink water every 15 to 20 minutes.

Humans need water to survive, but many communities do not have good access to clean water.

Access to Safe Water

Clean drinking water is a basic human need. The **United Nations** states that access to water is a human right. However, billions of people around the world have trouble accessing this precious resource. In some communities, the local water source is **polluted**—it has bacteria and dangerous substances that will make people sick. Some people must travel great distances to collect water. Many parts of the world are experiencing severe **droughts** and water shortages.

In many communities in the developing world, women must walk long distances every day to collect water for their family.

Meet some CHANGE MAKERS

Water For People

Water for People is a **nonprofit organization** that uses empathy to guide its projects around the world. In 2016, the team at Water for People helped Marie Claire Mukayiranga and her village in Rwanda by installing a pipe and tap for clean water. Before that, Marie Claire spent 4 hours every day walking long distances to collect water. That meant she had less time to do other important tasks, such as caring for children and taking care of the animals they rely on for food. When her children helped her carry water, they would be late for school. Water For People keeps stories of users like this in mind when they develop water systems for communities. By learning about Marie Claire's challenges, they found that a local water tap solves her problem. Now, she has easy access to clean water.

Water for People designs user-focused solutions to help women like Marie Claire access clean water in their community.

CASE

Access to Clean Water at Shoal Lake 40 First Nation

The First Nations are the Indigenous peoples, or the original inhabitants, of Canada. Bands, or self-governing communities of First Nations people, are usually located on **reserves**. The Ojibwa or Ontario Saulteaux people who live on the Shoal Lake 40 reserve in Ontario and Manitoba have followed a boil water advisory for 20 years. This means they must boil the water that comes from their taps to make sure it is safe.

Because the people of Shoal Lake 40 do not have good access to clean water, they are vulnerable to disease, and boiling water takes a lot of time and energy. The residents are frustrated and exhausted.

They are hopeful that a new **water treatment plant** will be built, but so far nothing is being done to provide them with clean water. Community members know that access to clean water is a human right. They want the government to listen to them and act on their concerns. They also want to be included in discussions and decision making about safe drinking water on their reserve.

Some Shoal Lake 40 community members participate in protests to bring attention to the problem. They believe the government has not met the terms of previous agreements, called treaties, to support First Nations.

The community of Shoal Lake 40 is not alone.

- As of fall 2016, there were 151 drinking water advisories across Canada in First Nations communities.
- Some First Nations communities must rely on bottled water—boiling the water still doesn't make it safe.
- 30 to 35 percent of homes on American Indian reservations in the United States get their water from untreated and unsafe sources, such as shallow wells.

The Design-thinking Process

Empathy What barriers to clean water does the community of Shoal Lake 40 face? How does this barrier affect their lives? What are the hopes of this community?

Define POV After you have used empathy to understand the Shoal Lake 40 community's point of view, define their needs. Create a POV question that helps you begin to solve their problem.

POV QUESTION PROMPT: **How might we ... ?**

CASE

The Flint Water Crisis

Fifteen-year-old Marzell Richmond and his family are from Flint, Michigan, which has experienced a major water crisis. In 2014, the residents of Flint learned that their tap water was contaminated, which means it was polluted and unsafe to drink. The water made many people very sick.

When the tap water in Flint, Michigan, became contaminated, the community had to drink bottled water, which was delivered by members of the National Guard.

At first, the government ignored the concerns of residents about the contaminated water, and information about the contamination was kept from the public. The problem is now being fixed, and the government provided water filters to residents, but many of these do not work.

Like others, Marzell still refuses to drink tap water in case the filters are not working properly. Marzell and his family use bottled water for drinking and cooking. But his family still uses tap water for bathing, and some of them have skin rashes. Marzell's family and many other residents feel hopeless and depressed that this might just be their new way of life. It has been many years since the contamination first happened, but Marzell, his family, and others in his community are still struggling. Marzell wishes others were aware that the water in Flint is still a problem for many people.

Since their concerns were ignored at first and evidence of the contamination was kept from them, many people in Flint do not trust the authorities.

Marzell and his family are not alone.

- The state of Michigan plans to replace the pipes that connect all residents to a safe water source by 2020.
- In November 2016, 90 percent of homes on Flint's water system had free filters installed, but more than half of the filters had problems.
- Interviews with 100 Flint residents in 2016 show that more than two years after learning their water was contaminated, they still experience the effects. After getting painful rashes on her skin, 16-year-old Iyanna Webb still used bottled water to bathe. She is one of many.

The Design-thinking Process

Empathy What barriers to safe water do Marzell and his family face? How does it make them feel?

Define POV After you have used empathy to understand Marzell's point of view, define his needs. Create a POV question that helps you begin to solve his problem.

POV QUESTION PROMPT: **How can we create a way to ... ?**

CASE

Need for Clean Water in Rwanda

Nadia, a teenager in Rwanda, has only a dirty swamp as a source for water. Like many Rwandans, her health is at risk because she does not have access to treated and cleaned water.

Nadia walks to a swamp where she collects contaminated water and carries it back to her village. This takes a lot of her time. The walk is even harder for Nadia because she is pregnant. She needs more time to work and earn a living to support her son. Nadia believes that village children get sick from the swamp water.

She thinks this is unfair. There is a water pump a short walk from her house, but it's broken. She wishes the pump worked and that clean water flowed from it.

Nadia and her community must rely on unsafe water sources such as the untreated water in this river.

Like Nadia, many Rwandans do not have a safe source of water.

- In Rwanda, 5 million people do not have access to safe water.
- More than 4 million Rwandans do not have a toilet. This means that human waste often makes its way into swamps, rivers, and other bodies of water.
- More than 900 children around the world die each year from diseases caused by unsafe water.

The Design-thinking Process

Empathy What barriers to safe water does Nadia face? What does Nadia think and feel about her situation?

Define POV After you have used empathy to understand Nadia's point of view, define her needs. Create a POV question that helps you begin to solve her problem.

POV QUESTION PROMPT: **How can we improve … ?**

Design Thinking in Practice

Accessing Clean Water

How can we help people have access to clean water?

It's time to put design thinking to work. Look back at the three users facing problems in this section:

1. The First Nations community of Shoal Lake 40 must boil their water and do not think the government is listening to or acting on their concerns.
2. Marzell Richmond and his family in Flint, Michigan, are still dealing with the 2014 water crisis. They get skin rashes from bathing in tap water and are still drinking bottled water only.
3. Nadia has no access to clean water in her village in Rwanda. She must walk far distances only to collect contaminated water to drink.

Which student or community would you like to help? Choose either the Shoal Lake 40 community, Marzell, or Nadia and use the design-thinking steps to create a solution to their problem.

Empathize

Empathize to learn more about the user's point of view:

- Ask questions about their needs.
- Learn more by watching videos and reading articles.

Define

Use the POV prompt from the case study to define your user's need.

Ideate

It's time to brainstorm! Draw, sketch, or write down as many ideas as possible. Organize your ideas and select one for the next stage

Prototype

Create a prototype of your idea—keep it simple, cheap, and easy. Remember that your prototype should be an experience.

Test

Show, don't tell—test your prototype with your peers to get feedback

Reflect

Reflect on the results of your test.

- Has your prototype met the needs of the user?
- What can you change?

Reflect on the design-thinking process.

- What did you learn?
- What could you do differently?

Now, improve your prototype through another iteration of the process. When you are happy with your solution, share it with your peers.

What's Next for Designing Healthy Communities?

As more people learn about design thinking, it continues to evolve. Design thinking is improving the lives of people in communities all over the world.

As our population increases, we will continue to face problems that affect human health. When future problems become more complex, design thinkers will help people find solutions that work because of their user-centered approach. Design thinking can make us more hopeful about future problems affecting human health. In Raleigh, North Carolina, the Community Food Lab is using design thinking to create systems, programs, and small businesses that help bring healthy food to the city's residents.

Leaders in Design Thinking

There are many organizations that run design-thinking programs. The Henry Ford Learning Institute and the Henry Ford Academies train educators in design thinking and run camps for students. Stanford University is creating innovative learning experiences for design thinkers and real-world projects. Stanford graduates created Noora Health, a program that helps hospital patients in India with at-home recovery. School Retool has a "Shadow a Student Challenge" that allows teachers and administrators to follow, or "shadow," students to learn how their experiences at school could be improved.

Learning More

Academy of Nutrition and Dietetic
Resources for teens so that they can make healthy food choices.
http://www.eatright.org/resources/for-teen

Henry Ford Learning Institute
Read about programs in design thinking for students, workplaces, and organizations.
https://hfli.org/what-is-design-thinking/

Practical Action
Information about Practical Action's floating gardens project.
https://practicalaction.org/floating-gardens

Katie's Krops
Students are helping to solve a hunger issue in their community.
https://www.katieskrops.com

The David Suzuki Action Plan
Information on how people can help end the water crisis in First Nations communities.
http://action2.davidsuzuki.org/water

This Girl Can
A campaign to get girls and women interested in fitness.
http://www.thisgirlcan.co.uk

Water for People
An organization that uses empathy to understand people's water needs and come up with solutions for them.
https://www.waterforpeople.org

WE Charity
An organization that uses empathy to solve problems affecting people's health and safety.
https://www.wecharity.org/about-we-charity/about-us/

Bibliography

Introductory Material

Kreinbring, Lisa. "What is Design Thinking?" Henry Ford Learning Institute, June 19, 2015. https://hfli.org/what-is-design-thinking/

"Our Impact." Stanford School, 2016. https://dschool.stanford.edu/our-impact

"Where We Work—Haiti." WE Charity, 2018. https://www.we.org/we-villages/where-we-work/haiti/

Project 1: Need for Active Living

Atkin, A. J., Corder, K., Morton, K.L., Suhrcke, M., and E.M.F. van Sluijs. The school environment and adolescent physical activity and sedentary behaviour: a mixed-studies systematic review. Dec. 18, 2015. http://onlinelibrary.wiley.com/doi/10.1111/obr.12352/full

Colangelo, Lisa L. & Ben Chapman. "Hundreds of city schools lack certified gym teachers, indoor space for exercise." *NY Daily News*. May 5, 2015. http://www.nydailynews.com/new-york/city-schools-lack-gym-teachers-indoor-exercise-space-article-1.2210230

"Constantly Connected: Adverse Effects of Media on Children & Teens." American Academy of Pediatrics, Oct. 7, 2016. https://www.healthychildren.org/English/family-life/Media/Pages/Adverse-Effects-of-Television-Commercials.aspx

"Current Physical Activity Guidelines." Centers for Disease Control and Prevention, Nov. 29, 2016. https://www.cdc.gov/cancer/dcpc/prevention/policies_practices/physical_activity/guidelines.htm

"Facts & Statistics: Physical Activity." US Department of Health & Human Services, Jan. 26, 2017. https://www.hhs.gov/fitness/resource-center/facts-and-statistics/index.html

Gavin, Mary L., MD. "Special Needs Fact Sheet: Spina Bifida." Nemours. February 2015. http://kidshealth.org/en/parents/spina-bifida-factsheet.html

Godman, Heidi. "Regular exercise changes the brain to improve memory, thinking skills." Harvard Medical School, April 9, 2014. https://www.health.harvard.edu/blog/regular-exercise-changes-brain-improve-memory-thinking-skills-201404097110

"Go where women are: Insight on engaging women and girls in sport and exercise." Sport England, https://www.sportengland.org/media/10083/insight_go-where-women-are.pdf

"Physical Activity Among Youth." Centers for Disease Control and Prevention, Nov. 29, 2016 https://www.cdc.gov/cancer/dcpc/prevention/policies_practices/physical_activity/youth.htm

Shields, Nora, and Anneliese Synnot. "Perceived barriers and facilitators to participation in physical activity for children with disability: a qualitative study." National Center for Biotechnology Information, Jan. 19, 2016. https://www.ncbi.nlm.nih.gov/pmc/articles/PMC4717582/

"This Girl Can." Sport England, 2018. https://www.sportengland.org/our-work/women/this-girl-can/

This Girl Can http://www.thisgirlcan.co.uk

"Where We Stand: Screen Time." American Academy of Pediatrics,

Nov. 11, 2016. https://www.healthychildren.org/English/family-life/Media/Pages/Where-We-Stand-TV-Viewing-Time.aspx

"Youth Risk Behavior Surveillance." Centers for Disease Control and Prevention, June 21, 2016. https://www.cdc.gov/mmwr/volumes/65/ss/ss6506a1.htm

Project 2: Need for Healthy Food

"Child Hunger facts." Feeding America. http://www.feedingamerica.org/hunger-in-america/child-hunger-facts.html

"Dining on Time." American Diabetes Association, Sept. 26, 2017 http://www.diabetes.org/food-and-fitness/food/what-can-i-eat/food-tips/eating-out/dining-on-time.html

"Find out about our simple ideas." Practical Action, 2018. https://practicalaction.org/media/view/48994

"Floating gardens." Practical Action, 2018. https://practicalaction.org/floating-gardens

"Growing Communities." Practical Action, 2018. https://practicalaction.org/bicas

"Hunger and Poverty Facts." Feeding America. http://www.feedingamerica.org/hunger-in-america/hunger-and-poverty-facts.html

"Infographics." American Diabetes Association, Feb. 1, 2016. http://www.diabetes.org/diabetes-basics/statistics/infographics.html

"Ten Things You Might Not Know About Diabetes." Joslin Diabetes Center. http://www.joslin.org/info/10_Things_You_Might_Not_Know_About_Diabetes.html

Katie's Krops https://www.katieskrops.com

"Malnutrition." World Health Organization, May 2017. http://www.who.int/mediacentre/factsheets/malnutrition/en/

"Nepal." Action Against Hunger, 2017. https://www.actionagainsthunger.org/countries/asia/nepal

"School and Diabetes." Youth Health Talk.org, December 2017. http://www.healthtalk.org/young-peoples-experiences/diabetes-type-1/school-and-diabetes

"Top 10 Things You Need to Know About the 2015–2020 Dietary Guidelines for Americans." Office of Disease Prevention and Health Promotion. https://health.gov/news/dietary-guidelines-digital-press-kit/2016/01/top-10-things-you- need-to-know/

"Top Facts About Hunger in Nepal." World Food Programme, 2018. https://www.wfp.org/stories/top-facts-about-hunger-nepal

"Types of Diabetes." Canadian Diabetes Association, 2018. https://www.diabetes.ca/about-diabetes/types-of-diabetes

"World hunger again on the rise, driven by conflict and climate change, new UN report says." World Health Organization, 2017. http://www.who.int/mediacentre/news/releases/2017/world-hunger-report/en/

Project 3: Need for Clean Water

"About." Shoal Lake #40, 2016. http://www.sl40.ca

Boyette, Chris. "Michigan and Flint agree to replace 18,000 home water lines by 2020." *CNN*. March 27, 2017. http://www.cnn.com/2017/03/27/us/flint-settlement/

"Flint Water Crisis Fast Facts." *CNN*, Nov. 28, 2017. http://www.cnn.com/2016/03/04/us/flint-water-crisis-fast-facts/index.html

Hanna, Jason. "Flint water crisis: Deliver bottles to homes, judge rules." CNN. Nov. 11, 2016. http://www.cnn.com/2016/11/11/health/michigan-flint-water-crisis/

Lukawiecki, Jessica. "Glass Half Empty? Year 1 Progress Toward Resolving Drinking Water Advisories in Nine First Nations in Ontario." David Suzuki Foundation, Feb. 2017 http://davidsuzuki.org/publications/reports/2017/DrinkingWaterAdvisory/

Mullen, Mary, and Jo Ellen Shield. "Water: How Much Do Kids Need?" Academy of Nutrition and Dietetics. May 2, 2017. http://www.eatright.org/resource/fitness/sports-and-performance/hydrate-right/water-go-with-the-flow

"Rwanda." Water Aid. http://www.wateraid.org/au/where-we-work/page/rwanda

"Short-term drinking water advisories: First Nations south of 60." Government of Canada, Nov. 30, 2017 https://www.canada.ca/en/health-canada/topics/health-environment/water-quality-health/drinking-water/advisories-first-nations-south-60.html

"Shoal Lake 40 celebrates start of on-reserve construction of Freedom Road." *CTV News*, June 30, 2017. http://www.ctvnews.ca/canada/shoal-lake-40-celebrates-start-of-on-reserve-construction-of-freedom-road-1.3484662

"Still Standing: 100 Flint residents dealing with daily pain of a poisoned water system." MLive Media Group. May 3, 2016. http://www.mlive.com/news/flint/index.ssf/2016/05/still_standing_100_flint_resid.html#4

"Water." United Nations. http://www.un.org/en/sections/issues-depth/water/

"Water Quality Study." Center for American Indian Health, 2018. http://caih.jhu.edu/programs/water-and-air-quality

"Women Driving Change." Water For People. https://www.waterforpeople.org/stories/women-driving-change#.Wd41YjaQLm0

Young, Molly. "Faces of Flint: Marzell Richmond." MLive Media Group. 2017. http://www.mlive.com/news/index.ssf/page/faces_of_flint_marzell_richmond.html

Glossary

aerobic Exercise (such as walking, jogging, and swimming) that lasts for several minutes or longer and strengthens the heart and lungs is called aerobic, because it works the system that moves oxygen around the body

blood sugar The concentration of glucose or sugar in blood

brainstorm A group discussion to generate ideas

diabetes A disease that make it difficult for the body to regulate the amount of sugar in the blood

disabilities Conditions of the body or brain that limit movement or activity

drought When a region does not get enough rain

failing forward Using feedback about mistakes to move forward in the design process

malnutrition A condition of the body that happens when someone does not eat enough nutritious food

nonprofit organization An organization that does not make a profit from its efforts—after expenses are paid, all money goes toward the public interest.

nutrients Substances in food—vitamins, minerals, fats, carbohydrates, and proteins—that the body needs to be healthy

obesity Being very overweight and having too much body fat

polluted Contaminated with unclean or toxic substances

process A series of steps taken to achieve a goal

processed food Foods that have been changed often by unhealthy added ingredients such as salt and sugar, or by preparation method, such as deep frying

reserves In Canada, land set aside for and governed by First Nations peoples. In the United States, federal Indian reservations are areas of land reserved for and governed by tribes of Native Americans.

role-play Acting out situations to learn about them

spina bifida A birth defect of the spine that can limit movement of the legs

storyboard A series of drawings that maps out a story, usually for making a video or cartoon

survey Collecting answers to a list of questions from many people

synthesize To bring together or combine information

type 2 diabetes The most common type of diabetes, when a person's body does not have enough insulin (the hormone needed to regulate sugar) or cannot use insulin effectively. Type 1 is when the body does not have insulin.

United Nations An organization that works to create cooperation, order, and peace around the world

water treatment plant A building or factory in which pollutants from water are removed before being used

Western Hemisphere The half of Earth that includes North and South America and all surrounding waters and islands

whole food A food that is natural and has not been changed with added sugar, salt, or chemical additives

Index

active living 20–27
aerobic activity 20

Bangladesh, flooding in 9
brainstorming 12–13, 27, 35, 43

communities, defined 7

defining user needs 6, 10–11
design thinking
  about 4
  and clean/safe water 39, 40, 41, 42–43
  and diabetic students 31–32, 34
  and food 31, 32, 33, 35
  and healthy communities 7, 44
  leaders in 44
  and physical activity 23, 24, 25, 26–27
  process 6–7
diabetes 31–32
disabilities, persons with 21, 23–24, 26

empathy
  about 6, 8–9
  and clean/safe water 39, 37, 40, 41, 43
  in design thinking 4, 6, 8
  and diabetic students 32
  and healthy food 29, 31, 35
  and hunger in Nepal 33
  and persons with disabilities 24
  and physical activity 21, 23, 25, 27
  prototype testing and 16
  reflecting and 18

failing forward 17
feedback 6, 16, 17, 18, 21, 27, 35, 43
First Nations communities, water in 38–39
Flint water crisis 39–40
floating gardens 9
flooding 7, 9
food
  access to 4, 7, 11, 28, 30–31, 34–35
  healthy 28–35
  snacks for diabetic students 31–32

Haiti, clean/safe water in 5
healthy communities
  about 7
  access to requirements for health 7
  active living and 20–27
  healthy food and 28–35
Henry Ford Learning Institute/ Academies 44
hunger 29, 30, 32–33, 34
hydration 13

ideation
  about 6, 12–13
  and clean/safe water 43
  and healthy food 35
  and physical activity 27
iterations 6, 27, 35, 43

Katie's Krops Dinner 29
Kielburger, Craig and Marc 5

malnutrition 29
mindset 7
Mukayiranga, Marie Claire 37

natural disasters 7
needs
  defining 10–11, 18
  and design thinking 6
Nepal, hunger in 32–33
Noora Health 44
nutrients 28

obesity 24

physical activity 20–27
  design thinking in helping 26–27
  insufficient space, at school 25
  people with disabilities and 23–24
  sitting/screen time and 22–23
point of view (POV)
  about 6
  and clean/safe water 39, 40, 41, 43
  defining 10–11
  and diabetic students 32
  and empathy 8
  and healthy food 31, 35
  and hunger in Nepal 33
  and persons with disabilities 24
  and physical activity 23, 27
  in prototype testing 16
  and school space for physical activity 25

Practical Action 9
prototypes
  about 6, 14–15
  and clean/safe water 43
  and healthy food 35
  and physical activity 27

Raleigh, NC, Community Food Lab 44
reflecting
  about 6, 18–19
  and clean/safe water 43
  and healthy food 35
  and physical activity 27
Richmond, Marzell 39–40
Rwanda, water in 41

School Retool, "Shadow a Student Challenge" 44
schools, space for physical activity 25, 26
sitting/screen time, and physical activity 22–23, 26
spina bifida 23–24
Stanford University 44
surveys 13, 17
synthesizing 10

testing, of prototypes
  about 6, 16–17
  and clean/safe water 43
  and healthy food 35
  and physical activity 27
This Girl Can 21

users, of design thinking 4

water
  clean/safe 5, 7, 36–43
  daily needs 36
  and health 36
  and hydration 13
  in Nepal 33
Water for People 37
WE Charity 5, 12

About the Author

Sheri Doyle is an author and editor who has written more than 20 books on a variety of topics, including language arts, geography, history, social science, and the arts. She writes both nonfiction and fiction for kids and teens.